LAYING OUT THE BODY

I Nia a Alice Megan

LAYING OUT THE BODY

Lucien Jenkins

SEREN BOOKS

SEREN BOOKS is the book imprint of
Poetry Wales Press Ltd.
Andmar House, Tondu Road, Bridgend, Mid-Glamorgan

©Lucien Jenkins, 1992

Cataloguing in Publication Data for this
title available from the British Library

ISBN: 1-85411-070-5

All rights reserved. No part of this publication may be reproduced,
stored in a retrieval system, or transmitted at any time or by any means, electronic,
mechanical, photocopying, recording or
otherwise without the prior permission of the author.

*The publisher acknowledges the financial assistance of the
Welsh Arts Council*

Typeset in 11 point Palatino by The National Library of Wales, Aberystwyth
Printed by John Penry Press, Swansea

Cover painting: Equus: Figure and Horse II by Denis Curry

courtesy of West Wales Arts Centre

Contents

I

9 Ginkgo
10 Upright
11 Egg
12 Less
14 Squib
15 Cockaigne
16 The Eye
17 Release
18 The Cat
19 Correspondences
20 The New World

II

21 Skins
22 A Triumph
23 A Woman Crying in Hackney
24 The Hanged Men
25 Landscape Into Art
26 Wisdom
27 Couple
28 The Dog
29 Shod
30 Blue Notes
31 Sharp
32 *An Engraving*
32   On Ken, Getting Out Of The Bath
33   Drawn
34   A Nativity
35   His Death
36 Above The Roof, The Sky
37 Hope Gleams

III

- 38 1611
- 40 Eclogue
- 41 Leafing
- 42 An Undertaking
- 43 Going Halves
- 44 After Wisdom
- 46 The Enclosure Acts
- 47 Script
- 48 *Speaking In Tongues*
- 48   Tongue
- 49   Welch
- 50   Words
- 51   Locative

IV

- 52 Emma
- 54 Guillaume IX
- 56 For Arnaut Daniel
- 57 For Dafydd ap Gwilym
- 58 The Holy War
- 60 The Love Song Of T. Stearns Eliot
- 61 La Folie Tristan
- 63 The Archaic Torso Of Apollo
- 64 Leda
- 65 Laying Out The Body

V

66 *An Altarpiece*
66   The Donors
67   Eve
67   Adam
68   Eden
69   Eve expecting Cain
70   God in the Middle Ages
71   An Annunciation
72   The Unicorn
73   A Nativity
74   Heaven
75   Adam
76   Eve

77 Acknowledgements

I

Ginkgo

You had it all your own way once.
Now, with your butterfly leaves,
you are alone.
Your family exists
only in stone memories.
Everywhere the late arrivals on the scene
spread, colonised and outgrew you.
You remained in China, an error
no one had remembered to rub out.

You stand in parks now, a survivor,
a tree from before there were trees.
You are slight, robust, gentle
and know too much.
Your roots grow down into sorrow.

Upright

We walk all over them, our feet.
We never asked their permission.

Early on we are lifted up.
Our feet, still soft, must take our weight.

When did we find out that standing
we were able to see further?

Was it because we missed the trees
when we went out to the grasslands?

We raised our faces from the earth
our sense of smell abandoned us.

We hold the delicate balance
upright as the needle of poised scales,

quivering as equal desires
insistently nag on each side.

Hands started by holding branches
and went on to play with the grass.

Now our hands have grown arrogant
and couldn't walk if you asked them.

Feet meanwhile remain symbolic
of humility and service.

Soles face the ground day after day
in their unremitting labour.

Their fingers are undeveloped
so that they cannot grasp ideas.

They have never questioned their fate.

Egg

The egg is an unbroken code
solving itself.

Inside, silent and shut away
like a monastery, everything
is dividing.

Like a locked, walled garden, the egg
turns its back on you however
much you turn it round in your hand.
All decisions are being made
in camera.

The egg now holds a prisoner
who hears through the breathing eggshell
rumours of freedom, of flying.
He is growing fast and his growth
is his secret weapon. He pecks
the prison wall. His chisel beak
breaks through.

>   The shell, abandoned now,
lies in two halves. Discarded crowns.
A broken code.

Less

The Earth shrank slowly at first,
Early reports were supressed
and the rumours not believed.

All carried on as before.
The Earth's anorexia
seemed to alarm nobody.

As the shrinking continued
things were closer together.
Open space was hard to find.

When Warsaw met Leningrad
everyone tried to behave
as if this were quite normal.

In Japan it was agreed
that if everyone stood still
no one would fall into the sea.

In the Atlantic, fishing
boats found themselves run aground.
Cross channel ferries were squashed

as the channel grew slimmer.
Territorial disputes
arose as nations withered.

Then the pace quickened.
Gravity grew less.

Things started falling.
Oxford Street got lost.

The attempt was made
to tie down Heathrow

but the cables snapped.
The sky became full

of objects falling
away from the Earth.

Then it was noticed
nothing had been heard

from France for some time.
Whole populations

simply disappeared.
The last survivors

desperately tried
to keep holding on

but the earth
now the size

of a plum
escaped them.

As they fell
they could see

the debris
of the shrunk

Earth, slowly
spinning round.

Squib

He lit up like a magnesium flare.
Everything went blue-white.
Not so bright, we complained.

You could read by him, take photographs.
The neighbours rang the doorbell:
the light was coming through the wall.

By now he was as good as a distress signal
sent up by a ship
and getting brighter.

Listen, we said,
calm down, stop to consider,
are you sure about this?

We were visible for miles:
the whole town was now merely
his lampshade.

We evacuated.
From the hills we watched
as he burnt himself out.

When we went back in
there were shadows on the walls.
Some things just weren't there any more.

When we found him
he was narrow and dark,
ordinary and left over.

We made him comfortable
but he didn't notice.
He had done it.

Cockaigne

When they beached the currach
   and walked inland
the castle wall was crystal
   the houses not timber but marble
and gemstone studded.
   There was a banquet laid
and no one to eat it but them.
   They fled from the hall
and sat by the river — fish
   leapt from the water into their hands.
When they hid in the wood
   pigs stopped rooting for acorns
and rushed over, stretching their necks
   for the knife's edge.
They hurried across the meadow —
   all the way
larks dropped out of the sky
   like hail.
Weeping, weeping,
   they made their way back
to their boat of timber
   and oxhides
where the crew lay
   gaunt as maps.
They floated loose
   on the rising tide.
They rowed until the wind
   found their sail.
A goldfinch pursued them.

The Eye

Something made his eye catch fire
one day on his way to work.
Flames leapt out and scorched his face.

Passers-by saw it happen.
'Gracious!' they said. 'Do you see?
That man's left eye is on fire.

Whatever next? I must say —
one's eye on fire in the street —
it's indiscrete, don't you think?'

All the way to work he saw
people nudge one another.
He ignored the whole affair.

Something must have caught his eye,
something inflammatory.
Once ablaze it would not douse.

At work he concentrated
while his forehead was melting:
he refused to be sidetracked.

He flicked through the day's reports
with attention to detail.
His assistant seemed upset.

His whole head was a bonfire.
A decision was needful.
But he delayed, hanging fire.

Release

(For the Golden Lion Tamarin, bred in
captivity, now being returned to the forests.)

I sit on the ground
and will not grasp.

They are taking away my bars.
These were my bones, my code.

What shall I do with distance?
Freedom given is no freedom.

The trees stand like questions,
tree after tree: how shall I

walk into this syllogism?
Ground, wind, tree:

I have no place in their argument.

The Cat

Come, and on my heart's love laze
    with hidden claws, dearest cat,
and let me plunge into your lovely eyes
    of mingled metal and agate.

When my fingers idly toy
    with your head and twisting back
and my hands are drunk with joy
    at the touch of your electric

body, I see a woman. Her stare
    like yours, dear cat,
deep and cold, stabs like a spear

and from head to foot
    a subtle air, a dangerous perfume
swirls about her dark form.

(after Baudelaire, *Le Chat*)

Correspondences

Nature's church has living pillars
which sometimes mutter muddled words;
we journey through symbolic woods
which watch us walk and closely stare.

Like far off echoes which confuse
into a dark, deep unity,
big as night, with day's clarity,
perfumes, colours and sounds converse.

Perfumes as fresh as a child's skin,
sweet as an oboe, prairie green,
and others, rich, corrupt and proud,

infinitely expansive, loud,
like amber, musk, benzoin, incense,
sing the joy of spirit and sense.

(after Baudelaire, *Correspondances*)

The New World

Strange to one another always: the still
of the clothed fields and soon,
after one smiling afternoon,
her door not open to you, her hand cool.

Only among strangers, out of her reach
could you inevitably find,
with the foreign silence, that sound
of unmeasuring speech.

Travelling across the gaping continent,
the strange birds slipping always out of view,
you weighed your sentences. The new
world. The old ways. Was that what she had meant?

Always the old spoke in the parched
hills, calling up the dead, knowing the loss,
the stolen or offended God. Across
so bare a recitation you still searched

in measured familiar prose to guess
towards that undenying land
where you and she could stand
questioning as water, naked as trees.

II

Skins

> 'Stop the riots, stop the muggings
> put the British people first.'
> *National Front News* and *The Bulldog*

1. Heads shaven to helmets butting the sky
   they stand stiff-faced in a line like a fence.

   Dignified as a row of cenotaphs
   they have stone dreams. Their language is all brick

   and lime mortar. Their monuments buckle.
   They are strapped and braced like buildings under strain.

2. They do not talk. Boots like heavy serifs
   fix them: capital letters in bold type.

   They stand like a printed word, a slogan.
   If they were fixed as a printer's cliché

   they would be happy, they think, while round them
   the brightly coloured world streams, spins and boils.

3. What they reject is the softness of flesh.
   They want to be all bone, unbending, stiff,

   a masculinity beyond all doubt,
   for flesh is doubt. They wear their certainty

   like a prepuce. Politics is their husk,
   a skin behind which they are soft as fruit.

A Triumph

The burnt out car
    sat in the road for days,
deeply unmoved,
    its view shattered,
its name blackened.

The boys had taken it
    to race against time
among the blocked off streets
    the bricked up Huguenot houses
and the walls sloganed with commands.

It had been a Triumph.
    No slave sat in the back
muttering death.
    They had been victorious
and cheered themselves like crowds.

At last they were good at something.
    They went from strength to strength
knowing all along
    how fire lay hidden in the car
as sparks in a flint.

A Woman Crying In Hackney

Your useless hands plunged deep into your pockets,
your head hanging,
you lean on the iron gate,
shaken with sobs,
the convulsive crying rocks you
and your large breasts shiver.

Quiet now, you take off your shoes
(they are trodden down and shabby)
and walk back into the house,
barefoot.

The Hanged Men

Your heads on one side like thoughtful children
and hands behind your back quite thoughtfully,
you hang in rows.

Always the onlookers, part audience
part congregation, stand expressionless
in their cheap suits,

while men in uniforms and caps, who try
to look as if they know a thing or two,
look serious,

hoping to persuade us that a man hung
in a tree is quite normal, quite clever.
Pleased with themselves

they seem happy to place this achievement
on record. Will they send the picture home
to be hung up?

Perhaps they think it is a work of art,
this man in a badly pollarded tree.
Meanwhile the line

grows longer and the dreaming, floating world
in which they drift like mobiles will not wake.
The audience,

gathered like drifting leaves, seem unsurprised
and unalarmed. The wind blows. They scatter,
light as ashes.

Landscape Into Art

Flat rich land the glaciers never gripped
pretending to a Dutch serenity
with Ruysdael cows, their pasterns deep in mud,
philosophising patiently at dusk,
their solemn, meadowed lives unfenced as thought.

Slowly the heron rises from the pool,
with awkward ugly beauty climbs the sky.
The F-16 and smooth F-111
teach us perspective's sharpest principles.

We graze this landscape. Paintings guard our eyes.
Hobbema lanes preserve the rule of law.
If hairs be wires, who combed this sleek barbed lock
across the soft brow of this almost hill?

Wisdom

> 'But false prophets also arose among the people,
> just as there will be false teachers among you.'

Good evening ladies and gentlemen. I
am the messiah, a Greek misnoma
for Messias, a.k.a. Maitreya.
I am the way and the truth and the life.
Despite my assistants carrying guns
(I have granted them a dispensation)
I oppose violence in all its forms.
What the world needs is a spiritual force.
I give classes in meditation, prayer,
massage, self-realisation and diet.
I have a degree in marketing from
a widely recognised polytechnic
in Panama. I would like to invite
all members of the audience freely
and without restraint to make donations
of not less than fifty pounds. This is used
for missionary and some relief work.
We only accept cheques if accompanied
by a bankers card. Please hand the money
to the ushers at the back of the hall
wearing blue uniforms and revolvers.
(See my pamphlet on generosity.)
Thank you for attending. Go peacefully.

Couple

Her clothing was comfortable,
There was room to move and she moved.
Bubbles rose in her and she giggled.
Her hands darted like swifts.

Salad-crisp, fresh, young,
you could have snapped her like a runner bean,
so slim, so young, so
undefended.

                While he

tall and grey as a church steeple, his clothes
a uniform. He wore them like a guard.

A wounded, sad obsession kept him there,
something forgotten, something important.

Jacket, shirt, tie all striped like a cage.
He was young, narrow shouldered
with white hands and small feet. His life
lay on him heavily as a lead roof.

The Dog

The dog is panting at your heels
    his tongue pursues you, rudely wet
your skin avoids its lechery
    and yet

the grinning dog won't let you go
    his muddy paws threaten your clothes
you stare round for his owner, how
    you loathe

the way he splashes through the mud
    as he comes sniffing at your skirts
he knows your smell   sickened
    you turn on him   beating   beating
    it hurts.

Something is bleeding. Your breathing
    is odd. What lies at your feet, dark
and with legs and open mouthed?
    The park

is closing as things done
    on evenings, in quiet rooms, years ago
pant at your heels and sniff and
    won't go.

Shod

1. Small as a pebble from a brook
   she slung herself in the world's face
   demanding its recognition.

   Shod in steel she battered pavements:
   on some nights you could see the sparks —
   a walking cigarette lighter.

   She hurled herself at my staircase
   wielding her two sticks like weapons.

   She leaned back in the chair, her legs
   stretched out. On her boots the steel gleamed.

2. Did birth joke with you, pulling your leg,
   leaving you to strut with crutches, iron shod
   like a carthorse, pulling the waggon God
   gave you for a body, grinning and drag-
   ging your full life, grappling with the unknown
   like a wrestler? When they explained, you were thrown.

   Did you begin planning that slow afternoon
   when you first heard the broken news? You saved
   the tablets you needed and one night braved
   your own darkness, leaving everyone
   to their separate, implicated lives. If
   you hesitated, what you thought or how
   you felt, I can't guess, as at last a slow
   tide caught you and you drifted off.

   (Mandy Dee: Born with cerebral palsy, developed
   multiple sclerosis, died by her own decision.)

Blue Notes

She sang.
          Afterwards
moving among them, grinning,
she nodded and joked as they
       praised
                  as they
      watched
                  as they
      paid
taking dollar bills, crisp clean limp dirty,
rolling them up tight as a cigarette
so she would lift her skirt,
put one foot on a chair, grinning
as they nodded and joked as they
slid the rolled money into her vagina
                  as she
      praised
                  as she
      watched
                  as she
      paid.
Jazz, jazz, jazz, roll those blue notes
                  for I
      praise
                  I
      watch
                  I
      pay.

Sharp

Narrow like a stamen
   and hair pollen yellow
he hung on his fishbone frame
   and would not allow

himself to be unnailed,
   needing to be pinned down.
Life hurtled like a gale
   past his life's filament.

He quivered like a needle
   pointing accusingly north.
Wearing his mind as a bridle
   he could not unclench his teeth

to speak. He kept his tongue sharp
   as a sheathed knife, afraid
it would cut his own throat. He hoped
   to hide it, biting the hidden blade.

An Engraving

1. On Ken, Getting Out Of The Bath

He hesitates, out of balance,
his balls swing in their loose purse,
big as plums under his penis,
now shrunk to a shy acorn.

He lifts one leg and sways wildly,
the skin flaps round his femur
like a sleeve but the wasted muscles
can no longer lift that bone.

The big lumpy foot splashes back.
He stands like a flamingo.
Now he attempts the other leg.
It is like walking on stilts.

One foot is lodged on the bath's rim,
the brown toes curl like a bird's.
The large thrust-out hands meet the floor —
he falls like a dockland crane.

The great quarrel of flesh and bone
is almost over and flesh
does not win. His boulder head rocks
as he finds his feet again.

2. Drawn

He is alone in his room now
    rehearsing for death
curled on his side, his knees drawn up
    under his sharp chin
making his last bed like his first
    his malt-dark eyes stare
and he waits, big-limbed and awkward
    like a staring chick.

Time has leached the strength from his legs.
    They cannot hold him.
Thin as a diagram, he seems
    sketched on the white sheet.
He draws his breath like water from a well.

3. A Nativity

Unstable, bruised from several falls,
   he slouches in his wheelchair.
His legs, ungovernable,
   now share

his hopelessness. His exhausted wife
   is sleeping. His puffy right hand
lies in his lap. He cannot stand
   and cannot write. His life

slips from his fingers like his pen.
   Death's tongue has licked him and he knows.
He will not walk again.
   His lips are dry. His mouth slurs.

Last night he fell out of bed
   and slept on the floor
with a scraped hand and a bruised head.
   He puzzles with the pen, unsure

how to grip it and writes shapes
   a ragged secret alphabet
of twists and slopes.
   Let it stand. Stet.

4. His Death

In the end he slipped away unnoticed.
His head thrust out like a gargoyle, his mouth gaped
as if the escaping spirit fled like rain.
We washed him and we laid him out. We dressed
him in his brightest clothes. He'd always hoped
that death would miss him, that he could outrun
the button moulder. Death came like a friend,
undoing 'this button'. How fast the flesh
darkened like a bruised potato and when we bent
him forward to ease his shirt round him, a rush
of stale air was pushed from his lungs in a faint
sigh. We sat with him, Sarah said Kaddish
as he lay, wrapped like a present. After prayers
came the sound of undertakers on the stairs.

Above The Roof, The Sky

Above the roof, the sky,
   so calm, so blue.
Above the roof, a tree
   waves to you.

A bell in that sky
   softly chimes.
A bird in that tree
   chants his rhymes.

God, this is life,
   that simple and quiet
sound you hear
   from the whispering street.

— Hey! You in there, crying:
   tell us the truth.
What have you done
   with your youth?

(after Verlaine, *Le ciel est, par-dessus le toit*)

Hope Gleams

Hope gleams like a wisp of straw in the stable.
Why fear the wasp, flying drunk, buzzing loud?
The sun always finds some break in the cloud.
Why didn't you fall asleep at the table?

Poor, pale soul, here's water, at least drink some,
cold from the well. And then sleep. Look, I'll stay
here and guard your dreams as you sleep today,
and you can sing like a child at bed time.

Midday strikes. Please, Madam, leave him alone.
He's asleep. It's strange, a woman's step can sound
so loud in such a restless, sleeping mind.

Midday strikes. Water's been sprinkled through the room.
Go, sleep. Hope gleams like a half-hidden stone.
Will we ever again see roses bloom?

(after Verlaine, *L'espoire luit comme un bri de paille*)

III

1611

It was a most unauthorised version:
you were sixteen and I was eleven.
The grasses gossiped softly, the wind freshened.
You felt like bread, hot and damp from the oven.

I stroked your fur like a cat's head. My hand
shook as my fingers found you open-mouthed.
The tongue of water lapped at the edge of the land.
Later, in church and cold and fully clothed,

crucifixes flew like a skein of ducks
on the hard white wall and the too-straight bricks
mounted, neat, sharp and hard as hymnal rhymes
to the flat ceiling. Outside, the box tombs

stood like glum houses in dead silence. Gulls
yelled from the cliffs, stone-heavy and cloud-light
as they plunged and wheeled. Afterwards, the dull bells
bit their tongues noisily as if taking fright
as darkness hurled towards us. Black rain fell
like a slammed door and the whipped sea's jaws bit
the soft cliff. Your father watched you. He could tell.
He spoke of Bathsheba and pride. And Hell.
Cold flames licked round your skirts like a dog. Your tight
starched blouse fooled no one. When he said: 'My own girl—
You stood and walked out. The baker's face was white,

uncooked looking. The congregation sighed
as you went out. We stood and sang loud
hymns: relieved, unnamed, hidden, while the tide
dragged at the shore like an ache and threw proud

sand on the wind which sowed it in our clothes
to itch like something true while time's lie soothes.

Eclogue

The crisis came — the petal-white semen
fell like confetti on the sudden wind.

The sky gaped like a yawn. The drenched fields dropped
slowly towards the swollen choked river.

At the field's edge the bagged potatoes stood
hunched. The seed potatoes lay and rotted.

I took the fork from the shed to dig beets.
Leaning on the haft I snapped a taproot

and a huge beet rose like a severed head.

Leafing

You were an unknown text and I skimmed:
what was I looking for as I thumbed

through your pages curled like new leaves
and heard your cursive breathing?

My pen plunged in that inkwell:
you were tight-faced, half fictional.

Your hair, black and kinked like gothic
script hedged round my scribbling prick.

I was too inspired to stop midsentence:
the poem fell in chaos on your tense skin.

We stared at this sudden Rorschach test
stuttered between your navel and your breasts.

An Undertaking

In the bedroom
he lifted up her arm and from

the curling finger tugged the lean gold hoop
entrusting it to me. A smear of soap

still showed on it from where she washed her hands
the night before. I couldn't find

a safe place for it. In the end
I threaded my handkerchief through this gold band

and knotted it like a memory.
Meanwhile among the mahogany

we tried to keep things measured
and balanced. But everywhere the dead

hands had left their fingerprints
like a careless burglar, all the ornaments

carried the trail, the tap
the kettle and the cups.

Going Halves

Something tore half my head away.
I never noticed it happen.
Then a dark screaming.

Ever since life has been simpler.
I can't remember what went wrong before.
Things are very simple.

I'm always on time for appointments now.
My handwriting has become legible.

When I look at people hurrying, angry.
I think: what they need

is having half their head blown away.

Afterwards it's simple. Simple as water.

After Wisdom

1. Across the way is haematology
     and down the corridor is X-Ray Dept.
   but this is Paulin Ward. Here the nurses
     in purple passion frocks and icing hats

   chat about Princess Anne and watch the police
     who're here to protect the royal visitor.
   Outside the trees burst like slow cool fireworks
     in a beauty beyond thought, so sure.

   The thermometer lies under my tongue
     and 'Nil by mouth' is hung above my head.
   Mr Anderson, his face scaffolded,
     is doing today's crossword in *The Sun*.

2. 'You'll have a bath at twelve and your pre-med
     at one. You're second on his list today.
   You'll be back here by half past three,' she said.
     'You'll still be half-asleep. You'll be in pain.

   You won't want any visitors till six.'
     I nod. 'Fine.' And sign the brief consent form.
   At my feet the irises are enflamed.
     We are four men. One does not speak but sits,

   one has to hold his tracheal tube to speak,
     one speaks a lot from an awkward, slanting mouth.
   I wait in my white gown. It has no back.
     Outside the plane trees shift in the wind's breath.

3. Envoi

My face swollen with outraged gums
I am back home.
From the open window come
the sound of breaking glass, the foreign scream
of a police car, from
time to time the glum
arguments of the young men as they strum
their car engines and the bam! Bam! Bam!
as the corrugated iron sheet on the slum
across the waste ground loosely slams

in the fitful wind.
Pain is a pathless land.
One step beyond its frontiers, I stand
and can't believe in the dark, dense land
through which I struggled so briefly to understand
what? That pain has no maps
and no rates of exchange, wound for wound:
one finger misshapen in a car door on a young hand,
the single pain as the brief short bone snaps.

The Enclosure Acts

Ta was common so we didn't say it.
My family belonged to too many classes
to risk relegation. Sod was common.
My father only said that when he dropped
a cigarette. Pop music was common
so we didn't listen to it. We weren't common.

My father called trunks 'bathers'. That was common.
At dinner he'd stand in front of the fire
between courses. That was very common.

Meanwhile we each owned our uncommon land,
fenced it in and worked it alone. We held
nothing in common and we had nothing
in common, digging behind tall hedges.

Script

Miss Coleman held up flashcards and we'd yell:
Yes! Good! House! Cat! Bell!

We practised our loops and joins with dip pens
in the staves of the buff exercise books.

My end of term report said: writing poor.
My fingers wore ink gloves. The letters hunched
in corners, mobbed each other, fell off lines.

Others, abandoning both page and pen,
patiently carved their names into the desk
or with a chalk (we had no spray cans then)
wrote 'Bum' unevenly up on some wall.

At breakfast I read the Kellogg's packet.
On the bus I read my orange ticket.
At school I read 'In case of fire break glass'.

I was given a fountain pen but ate it.
The report said: English good, writing poor.

Waiting for the bus I read the shop signs:
Coal Order Of ice was my favourite.

My parents' faces were lined and silent
as closed, densely written exercise books.
The rules were changing all the time and I
was lost. The report said: spelling still poor.

My father smashed the breakfast things one day.
The china fragments lay like bits of words
all through the dining room. My sister hid
and locked her door. He's mad, my mother said,
raving mad. I read the cornflakes packet:
Thiamine, niacin, riboflavin
and Mr Kellogg's name in special script.
My end of term report said: writing worse.

Speaking In Tongues

1. Tongue

Where will you go
as you spread yourself wider and wider
and will you find
you no longer recognise yourself,
tongue?

Dialect of a dialect
cobbled out of slave talk and soldiers' slang
and the half-hearted efforts
of the conquered to learn enough words
to understand orders
from yet more invaders
yet more men dressed in iron
building in stone.

Again the wooden houses burned
only to reinforce the point
that the invasion had happened
and the new rulers had come.

In you, copper and iron mix
and the commands
and the refusals
and the obedience
now lie moored, safe as ships.

You have travelled
barked orders yourself and taught
refusal and obedience and now
the plunder of the languages you killed
lies hoarded or squandered.

Von Humbolt found a parrot who could speak
a language — all the tribe were dead
and no one understood the parrot's words.

2. Welch

Let us take our history
fold it and tuck it in our wallet
like money

take the place itself
and hang it round our necks
like a charm.

Shall we examine the slate,
leaf through it for alibis?

Let us speak rather loudly about beer
and hills as though it were clever
and make much of the word waelisc.

***

Foreigned, my mouth plugged with English
like a too-big tongue half choking me
as you and your family giggled and bickered in Welsh,
I pulled on my boots and went into the rain.

Cymraeg, I muttered, going past the pigs
down to the sea, the corgi podging through the mud.
Saesneg: a mean, snap-jawed word
like a toad catching a fly with its tongue might say.
Saesneg!
While all the time my boots
mouthed in the soft-lipped mud:
Welch. Welch. Welch.

3. Words

How can I be fluent
    with your tongue
filling my mouth with new words,
    find a place among
your vocabulary of cliffs and cows?

My family's flat, clay language never lifted,
the tired river
drifted unlilting in its old age,
the sea waiting for it like a salt grave.

We did not leap. We lay in our shallow groove,
sliding between the cabbage fields, the sky
wide open above us like a great lie.

4. Locative

'Olive trees were extraordinarily abundant in the
medieval North...Whence do they come? From the
rhetorical school exercises of late Antiquity.'
                                    Ernst Robert Curtius

Unfamiliar trees stitched them in.
The olive, the palm, the vine, the cedar
bloomed on membrane pages.

In northern Europe, they and their thieved past
stayed resolutely indoors.
Pomegranates swelled in the library
figs grew plump in the undercroft.

They would not hear
the steady dripping of the cider press
an oozing clock.

They did not stand 'amid the alien corn'
but on familiar heavy northern soils
where sighing cattle gathered by the hedge.

IV

Emma

'What language was spoken by Queen Emma (d. 1052), daughter of Richard I, duke of Normandy, and wife first of Aethelred the Unready and second of Cnut the Great?'

                                                  J.C. Holt

Did you ever see a map
or did you never know where you were
as the men bought and sold you like land, like cattle
what kind of syntax
what kind of vocabulary
did you use
struggling to make demands
or did you give up
and wander among cold stone rooms
where the women sewed and whispered
their lumpy glutinous words
and never looked you in the eye.

Among those countries, those castles
when you dreamed
did you call out
and in what language
with what accent.

And when they came to you at night
smelling of goosefat
what could you say:
you knew his name and mispronounced it,
Aethelred, Cnut.
Were you more than a tract of land to him
as he ploughed you,
Aethelred, Cnut.

Or were you able
as the dip flickered
to understand his botched words
and tell him anything,
Aethelred, Cnut,
wandering among words.

Guillaume IX

Ferai un vers de dreyt nien.

They are painting faces in the trees again.
This place is cold. Damn winter. Damn rain.

I shall make a poem out of the void.
I shall not write about myself, no word
of being in love or youth, or manhood,
nothing like that.
I love to feel my horse sweat when I ride.
I love her heat.

I can hear them now, dancing by the church
through the graves. As a boy I went to watch,
crept down to the village, hid in the porch,
watched them join hands
with the dead, heard the singing, smelled the stench
of leaping bodies and trodden grass, such
sweetness. In the morning the dropped, plaited flowers
and the priest muttering 'Debauched! Debauched!
Selling themselves to darkness, the animal powers.'
Thin, angry, tanned.

I don't know how I came to be born
neither a smiling nor a sorrowing man,
neither a stranger nor anyone's friend.
One night a spell
was cast that made me who I am
on a tall hill.

Two hours till dawn
and still the rain drips onto Aquitaine.
My heart is torn
in two with sorrow, my body bruised with pain.
I pray both in Romance and in small Latin
that God will lighten me, will lift this burden

of idiot flesh, hung on me like a chain:
Christ set me free.
Am I awake or dreaming? The priest explains
God's mercy and how the hosts of heaven
will welcome me
all clad in light and the gates will open:

shall I believe again? No! I shall listen
to the slow persistent plodding of the rain,
its soft footfalls.
The restless dead now seek me in my chamber:
I hear them call,
I see their shadows dancing on the wall.

For Arnaut Daniel

I can hear the leaf fall
and see the wind sharpen the hazel.

Milk freezes in the bucket
half way between udder and breakfast.
The bracken is fox-red on the hills.

No one blames Life: she never steals,
just repossesses a few loans.

Perhaps happiness is unnatural,
an unrest into which Life rushes griefs
like a crack riot squad.

The hogs are brought in,
chubby with snouting up acorns,
grinning at their friends,
hoping for hazelnuts.

For Dafydd ap Gwilym

The priest, growing feathers,
squatted blinking in the hawthorn
while people, noisy as coins,
rattled below, dull and hard.

He was a thrush. His speckled chasuble
ruffled in the sharp wind.
He took his text from the thorns
and read its hedged black letters.

He read the lection, he spoke in tongues.
All round the coppiced hazels bled.

The Holy War

I have read *The Plain Man's Pathway to Heaven*.
I have read it.
But I am not a plain man.

   Look alive, trooper!
      Yessir.

Walk towards God, John.
Walk straight towards him.

I fell into Bedford river and would have drowned
with my fingers I plucked out an adder's sting
a man took my place in the war
and was shot for me
death has doors on every side
every milk-house, stable and barn
has doors opening into death's hall.
What shall I do?

I ring the church bells but they frighten me:
their yawning mouths roar and groan in the steeple,
their tongues hang down like a dog's in August.
How if one of the bells should fall?
What if the steeple should fall — and the bells
came howling after me like a pack of hounds?

To whom should I pray
to a hammered God?

Between Bedford and Elstow I command
the dry places in the road, give orders
to the puddles and have authority
over the dung and clay. The river dreams
and never lifts her head. Now on the bank
they are stripping the willow and weaving

hurdles, pressing mud into this lattice,
building cottages along the road.

   Trooper, have a care for your musket.
      Yessir.

We are made no more strongly than these walls,
the flesh pressed tightly in among these bones:
what do we hope to leave — iron shackles
and a tin fiddle to be our witnesses?
There is a fire burning in me now:
the tinder of my body is in flames
wherever I walk, terror makes me curse
I hold my face to try and stop the words
my tongue dances — I clap it in my fist.
The words are prisoners now — I have them caught
and am their cell: they hammer in my head.
I am a door and they would break me down.

The Love Song Of T. Stearns Eliot

'It was no summer progress
at that time of year,
the days short, the sun farthest off,
in solstitio brumali.'

It is not the unpaid debts,
with their whisper of dying leaves
that put their eye to the lattice
and try the latch quite softly.

Pity and duty surround me.
I, with Malacca cane and spats
and double-breasted suit and bowler hat,
offer the camera my cold, padlocked smile.

Something is lacking: shall I hide
here in this thorn-hedge while the soldiers pass,
a vague neighing of horses, rattle of swords
and far-off rumours of guns. And my wife's voice.

Perhaps at dinner I shall murmur jokes
about 'august caesurae' while they stare
uncomfortably at my green powdered face.
I am unwell. Bring me my coat. Good night.

La Folie Tristan

Tristan danced in the doorway
    Marc lurked on the throne.
He took no heed of the juggling
    he did not laugh at the clown.

Tristan danced in the courtroom
    where Marc sat inventing laws
he danced among the documents
    but the court didn't even pause.

Tristan danced in the chapel
    Yseut and her maid were at prayer,
incense and the fragrance of cattle
    hung heavy on the autumn air.

Tristan danced through the market
    below in the town square:
only a hen in a wicker cage
    recognised him there.

Tristan danced in the orchard
    over the rotting fruit,
the wasps rose from the apples
    and wove about his feet.

Tristan danced down the valley
    upon the fallen mast.
A pig raised his snout from eating
    and watched him tumble past.

Tristan danced to the moorland
    across the bitter peat.
The sodden black earth stained his skin
    and stones tore his feet.

Tristan danced over the cliff's edge
   to the sea's imperfect cadence.
The waves licked his wounds and whirled him
   deeper into the silence.

Yseut had finished praying.
   Marc had dispensed the law.
The royal couple moved across
   the blue slate floor.

Brengain watched them at dinner
   and watched as they went to bed.
The sounds of their snorting lust at night
   rooted like pigs in her head.

The Archaic Torso Of Apollo

We did not know his astonishing head,
eyes ripening like apples. But the torso
is lit by their gaze like the afterglow
of flame in a candelabra that flared

and still burns. Otherwise the swelling chest
could not blind you and in the light curve
of the loins a smile could never move
towards that centre where begetting rests.

Otherwise the stone would stand disfigured, cropped
under the shoulders' lucid sudden drop,
it would not gleam like a wild creature's fur,

nor would it come blazing out like a star
past its own rim. There is nothing here
which does not watch you. You must change all you are.

(after Rilke, *Archaïscher Torso Apollos*)

Leda

As the god entered, driven by what he lacked,
he was almost shocked to find the swan so fine;
he was confused, losing himself in the swan.
But soon his disguise drove him to the act

before he had yet tasted the still
untested self. And the woman, discovered,
knew him, the swan arriving, the lover,
and knew too: that one desire filled

him which she could not withstand,
nor could she hide what he wanted. Down he flew,
his neck thrust past her ever weaker hand

and in the beloved the god was lost, gone.
Then he exulted in his feathers. Through
her flesh, for the first time, he was a swan.

(after Rilke, *Leda*)

Laying Out The Body

They were accustomed to him. When they came
the kerosene lamp burned uneasily
in the dark wind. They did not know his name.
An unnamed man. They sponged his throat softly,

washing and chatting and knowing nothing
drove them to conjure a story for the man,
telling him his life. One broke off coughing
and left the vinegar-drenched sponge no more than

a moment on his closed mouth. They both paused:
from the hard-bristled brush in the other
woman's hand, water drops ticked, while his paws,
cramped queerly, were unmoved. He did not whisper
that he was not thirsty to the listening house.

Yet they had heard him and feeling ashamed
they set to work again, clearing their throats
while on the wallpaper of the unnamed
room, their shadows danced and twisted as if caught

under a hunter's net. They worked without a pause
to finish washing him. Outside the house
Night pressed her forehead to the window frame,
her gaze pitiless. Someone with no name
lay there clean and naked and giving laws.

(after Rilke, *Leichen-Wäsche*)

V

An Altarpiece

1. The Donors

Kneeling in double-side cloth
(the local product) with fur cuffs
and collar, he is slightly hunched
as if discussing a fresh loan.

His wife is tough, her book-like face
is full of undisguised suspicion:
life is a column of figures
and she is still adding it up.

Hands that have spent the day counting
money, feeling the weight of cloth,
look ill at ease lifted in prayer.

Their clothes are tidily folded.
But while they lift their eyes to God
his purse still hangs down heavily.

2. Eve

This flesh is wise: it feels the pull
of earth upon it. The soft droop
of her breasts and the downward curve

of her stomach show how full
they are and life is; this weight, heaped
upon braced, strong legs that heave

up that body's pondering load.

3. Adam

His face is soaked with thought: the full
knowledge has seeped in drop by drop,
flooding his mind. Now he must live.

The tide of his own actions pulls
him far out to sea. He had hoped
to look with new eyes: he must leave

now and not even choose the road.

4. Eden

Perhaps the embrace is the image of God,
the reconciliation of all we are
with all we cannot be. Life is so large:
why was I so well prepared for prison?
The cell so full, the small barred window high
in the wall, the pisspots in the corner
(we had one each) I was too shy to use.
I lay on my bed. I had the bottom bunk.
We dozed while John went through his magazine.
At last he chose one woman to tear out
and with four small seeds of blu-tack, she joined
his gallery, a rich harvest of flesh
he had gathered over his bunk. Women
stared out at him in rows, their swelling skins
a vision of a fuller, larger world,
a richer earth from which the plants leap up
vast breasts to fill and overflow his hands,
a guess to take Columbus in an eggshell
out of the world, dragging with him a crew
convinced that they had died and this new world —
the copper men, the gold, the strange bright birds —
were things articulated by a dream.
We lay in our cell, three men together
and chatted. The prison boomed with slammed doors.
There on the wall of the cell, the women
still stared, their adamant nakedness glowed.

5. Eve expecting Cain

I am swollen like a corm
and the autumn is kicking
in me now. I am no longer
myself, I have become only
an open door.

We have no past: there was simply
a long, disappearing present.
At the end of each day
a brooding, blank-faced sun
hangs at the world's rim
unforgivingly.

6. God in the Middle Ages

And they hoarded him in their hearts
and they wanted him to be and govern
and to hinder his travelling to heaven
they finally hung on him, like weights,

the load and burden of their cathedrals.
And that he should circle, was all they asked,
marking the trivial round and common task,
over his undivided numerals,

signing and indicating like a clock.
But suddenly he really began to turn
and fearing the chiming terror of his voice

the people of the city, now in shock,
left him, pendulum swinging, to run on
and fled the numbered staring of his face.

7. An Annunciation

The landscape was a voice
and when it spoke
something like fire
poured through me:
leaves spread over my hands
and my feet seemed
to root deeply
in the soft clay
by the pool's edge.
I could feel the rising
of a column of water
drawn through me continually.
Half of me was in leaf
and half in flame.

8. The Unicorn

God with his wooden arms flew through the night
and Saint Luke hedged with barbed wire and blackthorn
lowed discontentedly, solitary as a unicorn.
Perfection beckoned, dressed in candid white,

to the gathered children waiting in the square.
Inside there would be miracles. The stone
would weep and nod and solemn men in prayer
would weep and nod with her. The unicorn

would rush into the church pursued by hounds,
would leap into her lap and there be torn
to fragments, leaving her untouched, unwounded,
holding as if surprised, the single horn.

9. A Nativity

The goldfinch paused by the green canal
where the gasometer rose like a hollow crown,
burned like a flare on the littered ground
then flashed to the ridge of a moss-daubed wall.

The goldfinch paused on the child's fist
as he lay in his pram by the dull canal
while his mother drank from a can and all
round dumped cars rust.

10. Heaven

Here the land was always poor,
too full of streams,
shallow, slipping south to the river,
curled like a sperm at the sea's egg.

Some have collapsed here, poverty
has dug deep into them
and the crust of their lives
has caved in.

Some have outsmarted themselves,
they wear bright clothes
and assure you that having no money,
no future, no work is clever.

Some stand in the queue at the take away,
the clean counter, the orderly tables,
the crisp paper sack of tidy food
is sweet with the promise of heaven —

for surely this is heaven,
that the forests have been torn up like cardboard,
the beef herds slaughtered
and the earth's cloak of air torn

only to feed us, to please us,
a tribute to our importance, while outside
pigeons, limping like biblical beggars,
bicker over the litter of dropped bread.

11. Adam

He stands astonished on the steep cathedral,
that surge of stone, awestruck, beside the rose
window, at the apotheosis which chose
him and grew in him and set him down, all

of a sudden, in dominion over
these and these. He soars and enjoys his span
and he has made up his mind. The first man
who farmed, who did not know how to discover

a path from the full-rich finished Garden
of Eden, out into the new-made Earth.
God was hard to persuade. His one reply

instead of helping was to threaten
saying over and over, he would die.
But the man still answered: she will give birth.

12. Eve

She stands simply on the great cathedral,
that surge of stone, holding, beside the rose
window, the apple in the apple pose,
guiltlessly guilty now, once and for all

of the growing to which she gave birth
since she broke lovingly out of the ring
of eternity to go struggling,
young as a new year, over the Earth.

Ah, how she would have liked to have remained
longer with the animals in that land,
a witness to their reason and accord.

But she found the man had made up his mind,
she went with him, death was the journey's end;
and she had hardly begun to know God.

Acknowledgements

A number of these poems have previously appeared in: *Acumen, Argo, Iron, Litmus, Orbis, Other Poetry, Outposts, Poetry Review, Poetry Wales, The Rialto, Resurgence, Stand; The Bloodstream: Seren Poets One; Poetry Wales: 25 Years* (Seren Books). Sections 6, 11 and 12 of 'An Altarpiece' are translations from Rilke.